THE FANTASTIC FART BROTHERS'

BiG BOOK

OF

FARTY FACTS

AN ILLUSTRATED GUIDE TO THE SCIENCE, HISTORY, AND ART OF FARTING

by M.D. Whalen
illustrated by Des Campbell

First UK/international edition, published 2017

 Top Floor Books
imprint of stvdio media
PO Box 29
Silvermine Bay, Hong Kong

visit us at www.topfloorbooks.com

ISBN 978 962 7866 36 7

CONTENTS

INTRODUCTION

HOW MUCH DO you know about farts? They stink, they feel good, and some sour-faced people think they're rude. But farts are rather interesting things.

Fart jokes go back thousands of years. There's a religion that worships farts. People in the Amazon jungle fart to say hello. Farts have caused revolutions and almost started wars. Human farts are illegal in Africa and cow farts are illegal in California.

Fish fart. Astronauts fart even more. Even dead people fart. Farts can destroy the planet, but smelling farts can be good for your health.

Crack open a tin of bean dip, grab a fizzy drink and a bowl of onion soup, sit back, and toot your bum off at the windy and wacky world of musical gas.

SECTION ONE

FART SCIENCE

4

Fart Chemistry

FARTS STINK AND you can light them on fire. So what are they made of?

An average fart consists of:

- 59% nitrogen (N_2)
- 21% hydrogen (H_2)
- 9% carbon dioxide (CO_2)
- 7% methane (CH_4)
- 4% oxygen (O_2)
- 1% hydrogen sulfide (H_2S)

The smelly part is hydrogen sulfide. It is so powerful that, even though it makes up only 1/100 of a normal fart, one tiny poot can stink up a whole room. The British Army used concentrated hydrogen sulfide as a poison gas in the First World War. Maybe that's why baked beans are so popular in England: they're a secret weapon.

Hydrogen sulfide is also flammable, as are hydrogen and methane. Almost one third of a fart's contents can catch fire. You could roast a sausage with flaming farts...but would you eat it?

Finally, farts also contain oxygen, but not much. If you breathe pure farts, it will keep you alive for around 15 seconds, if the stink doesn't kill you first.

Faster than a Flying Fart

CAN YOU OUT-RUN a fart?

Scientists haven't yet studied the speed of farts, but some evidence shows that farts travel up 10 feet (3 metres) per second. Almost 7 miles (11 kilometres) per hour. Most people jog at around 8 miles (13 kilometres) per hour.

Does that mean, when you hear a fart, you have a chance to escape?

Not so fast!

At bum level, the wind from a fart might be that strong, but it obviously slows down right away as it pushes against the air around it.

So, that means you can just walk away, right?

Sorry, no.

Although a fart's wind speed might slow way down, the tiny stink molecules quickly spread among the other molecules in the air, in a process called diffusion. In a warm, still room, those molecules can travel around 800 feet (243 metres) per second. That's 545 miles (878 kilometres) per hour. Which is nearly the speed of a jet airliner.

Still think you can out-run a fart?

Gas Warfare

MANY ONLINE SOURCES claim that if you fart constantly, day and night, for 6 years and 9 months, enough explosive energy is produced to equal an atomic bomb.

Sorry, it isn't true.

That amount of intestinal gas, ignited all at once, would produce a fireball over 6 miles (10 kilometres) high, that that is still far less power than the smallest atomic bomb.

However, it is true that, theoretically, it would take only nine farts from every person on earth to produce the same power as a hydrogen bomb.

Let's all hope that there's never a World War Phew.

Fart Breath

HOW MANY FARTS are in the air? Let's do some arithmetic...

The average person farts 14 times in a day. Multiply that by 7.515 billion people on earth:

That's over 105 billion farts every day!

There are 86,400 seconds in a 24-hour day.

Do the division: that makes 1,217,708: way over one million farts *every second* of every day!

Then how much of the air we breathe is made out of farts?

According to a scientific study, the average human fart is a little over half a quart or half a litre (0.55687 quarts/0.527 litres) of gas.

Multiply that by 105 billion farts:

Nearly 15 billion gallons (55 billion litres) of farts are released into our atmosphere daily.

And that's just human farts. We didn't even add in dog, pig, cow, and—yes—termite farts.

Take a deep breath!

Fartometer

SCIENTISTS ACTUALLY MEASURE people's farts.

In 1940, researchers in Chicago invented a special tube which they inserted up a patient's rear end. Then they plugged the patient's bum shut. At the other end of the tube were thick rubber balloons which filled up as the subject tooted.

These days, a laboratory at Laurentian University uses electronic sensors to measure how much hydrogen sulfide is in the air. Since most hydrogen sulfide comes from farts, you know what they're studying.

And you thought science was boring!

Fart Medicine

FARTS CAN TREAT diseases!

Scientists have found that the stinky substance in farts—hydrogen sulfide—has possible health benefits for a number of conditions, including diabetes, heart attacks, strokes, and dementia. It does so by repairing mitochondria, the parts of our body's cells which produce energy and keep them—and us—feeling young.

In other words, consuming farts can make you healthier, stronger, and live longer!

Dr Mark Wood, from the University of Exeter in England, says:

"Although hydrogen sulfide is well known as a pungent, foul-smelling gas in rotten eggs and flatulence, it is naturally produced in the body and could in fact be a health care hero."

Another scientist, Dr Rui Wang of Laurentian University in Canada, goes even farther:

"If you don't fart, you die."

Fart Psychology

FARTS MAKE YOU happy.

You already knew that.

Russian scientists proved it by studying the natural body chemicals which create gas in your intestines.

They discovered that some of the molecules which cause gas act as *gasotransmitters* (yes, that's what they are actually called), which send signals to your brain. These signals affect depression and aggressive behaviour. Further studies could lead to a new treatment for depression.

Therefore, next time you're feeling down, cheer yourself up by sniffing some farts.

SECTION TWO

Blowiest Beans

MIRROR, MIRROR ON the wall, what's the fartiest bean of all?

Most studies agree on which bean packs the most poot. And the winner is...

- Soybeans!

Here are the runner-ups which give the next biggest blow, with the gassiest at the top:

- broad beans (lima beans)
- garbanzo beans (chick peas)
- navy beans
- pinto beans
- black-eyed peas

What about the least gassy beans?

The dark green kinds, like string beans, won't make much wind (so why bother to eat them?). Nor will jellybeans.

All beans lose their flatulent effect the longer they're soaked in liquid. That means tinned beans, the kind which are packed in water or sauce, cause less gas.

And less fun.

Fartiest Foods

WHO ABOUT OTHER foods besides beans? If you want a rip-roaring meal, here's a musical menu to choose from:

- **Methane-making Meat**

  beef, especially when cooked rare

- **Venting Vegetables**

  asparagus, brussels sprouts, broccoli, cabbage, onions, artichokes, peas, celery, sweet potatoes

- **Tooty Fruits**

  watermelons, blackberries, prunes, apples, mangoes, peaches, pears

- **Gassy Grains**

  barley, rye, wheat, flax seed

- **Cuttin'-the-Cheese Dairy**

  ice cream, buttermilk, cream cheese, ricotta cheese

- **Duck-quacking Drinks**

  sugary drinks, fruit juices, beer

Stink Sandwich

DID YOU EVER try pumpernickel bread? It's a German dark bread made from coarsely-ground rye...which, as you know, is one of the gassiest grains.

The original German meaning of *pumper* is "fart" and *Nickel* is an old German name for "little devil". So if you eat pumpernickel, you'll fart like the devil. Yes, that's really where the name comes from.

Pray for forgiveness to whoever is next to you when you eat a pumpernickel and onion sandwich.

Other Gas Sources

HERE ARE OTHER ways to increase your thunder down under.

- **Chew gum:** when you chew chewing gum, you swallow a lot of air. This passes through to the other end. Unfortunately, those farts don't stink.

  Unless you chew sugar-free gum! Sorbitol, a common artificial sweetener, stimulates the bacteria in your gut which produce normal nose peelers.

- **Suck hard candies:** Same with chewing regular gum, you're sucking in lots of air, but spewing out plain ordinary wind.

- **Drink fizzy drinks:** By now, you get it. The bubbles pass through your system, and will give you screaming howlers, though with barely enough odour to clear a room. But diet drinks, like sugar-free gum, can give you the putrid punch you need.

- **Eat quickly:** If you stuff your gut too fast, your body just wants to move it along. The sugars and starches in your food aren't fully digested and turn into gas.

SECTION THREE

Boy vs Girl Farts

DO GIRLS FART less than boys? Yes and no.

A study by fartologist Dr Michael Levitt has proven that when men and women eat the exact same food, a woman produces a smaller volume of gas. But that's only because female gas is more concentrated than the male stuff.

In other words, girls' farts are thicker than boys' farts, including the stinky part.

That means girl farts actually smell worse!

Dreamy Farts

PEOPLE FART MORE while sleeping. This is because our muscles are more relaxed, including the ones that normally hold farts in.

Here are some ways to avoid suffocating yourself or another person at night:

First, don't eat snacks or drink fizzy drinks before bed.

Second, don't lie on your belly, since your body weight pressures your intestines to push out air.

Third, drink water before sleeping, which calms your digestion.

But the number one best way to fart less in bed is:

Fart more during the day! Let it all blurt out! You'll make people laugh, you'll feel better, and you won't risk suffocation in a closed bedroom.

Underwater Farts

SCUBA DIVERS CANNOT pass gas at depths of 33 feet (10 metres) or deeper. This is because the water pressure is so great that the gut stops forming gas bubbles.

What if you fart while swimming in shallower water? Will releasing gas make you less able to float? Not really.

However, farting while diving can cause other problems:

Any underwater pressure will make your farts more concentrated, which also makes them more powerful. An underwater fart can actually rip a hole in your wetsuit. Then the force of the fart can make you shoot to the surface too quickly, which can cause decompression sickness.

But the worst danger is that sounds travel farther underwater: a massive fart explosion can attract sharks from far and wide!

Heavenly Farts

DEAD PEOPLE FART.

For up to three hours after death, human bodies have been known to continue burping and farting.

Now you know what all those clouds up in Heaven are made of.

FARTY ANIMALS

Fartiest Animals

WHICH ANIMAL IS the biggest farter on earth? You might guess it's your dog. Maybe you've heard that cows farts cause global warming. But by far the fartingest animal of them all is...

· Termites.

They may be tiny, but for their body size, they fart way more than us. And there are lots of them. Scientists estimate that the total farts released into the atmosphere by all termites on earth is 77 billion gallons (290 billion litres) per day. By contrast, all humans together release a mere 15 billion gallons (55 billion litres). We're out-farted five-to-one!

Next in line for most flatulent creatures are:

· Camels
· Zebras
· Sheep
· Cows
· Elephants
· Dogs (farting-most breeds: Labradors and Retrievers)

Humans rate somewhere below dogs. Maybe we should be eating more dog kibble.

Scientists set up a public database of animal farts (and pukes) at: goo.gl/szRRQE

Fart-Free Animals

IS THERE ANYTHING that doesn't fart?

Jellyfish don't, nor do sea anemones or corals. They don't have brains, either, so they don't know what they're missing.

Worms have brains, but there's one kind that doesn't fart, called the Pogonophoran Worm.

Birds don't fart, but only because they never need to. They don't even burp. Birds don't have the same kinds of gas-forming bacteria and chemicals in their guts as humans and other animals.

In conclusion, anyone who claims they don't fart is either a bird brain or has no brain at all.

Cows Fart at Both Ends

COW STOMACHS HAVE four sections. The first section breaks down the grass and grain they eat.

When it passes into the second section, it produces gas. This gas forms for a reason: they need to burp the food back up into their mouths, so they can chew it longer. Those burps are full of methane, just like farts.

Of course, after the food passes through all four sections of a cow's stomach and then the intestines, you can hear cow trumpets playing clear across a pasture.

But the funny thing is: there's more methane in their belches than in what toots out behind.

So you can truthfully say that cows fart from both ends.

Farting Ninja Elephants

ELEPHANTS FIGHT WITH farts.

They have huge stomachs which make them one of the top-farting animals on the planet. The average adult elephant farts around 265 gallons (1000 litres) of methane every day, enough to power a normal car for 20 miles (32 kilometres).

With all that ninja fart power, it's no surprise that they put it to good use. When one elephant gets another one angry, don't be surprised to see the victim fart in the first one's face.

Now we know why elephants' noses are so long: to avoid the stink.

Snake Farts

SOME SNAKES HISS. Some rattle. But when coral snakes want to scare you, they fart.

When they feel threatened, coral snakes release small popping poots to frighten away predators.

That means coral snakes can poison you without taking a single bite.

Fish Fart Language

HERRINGS SPEAK IN farts.

These silvery fish blow bubbles out their anuses, producing a high-pitched popping noise that only they can hear.

Biologists named this noise Fast Repetitive Tick, or FRT.

Unlike human farts, which make others run away, fish FRTs bring them closer.

Herrings only FRT after dark, to find each other and keep their schools together at night. Since no other sea creatures can hear the sound, herring can FRT as much as they like without attracting danger. Or laughs.

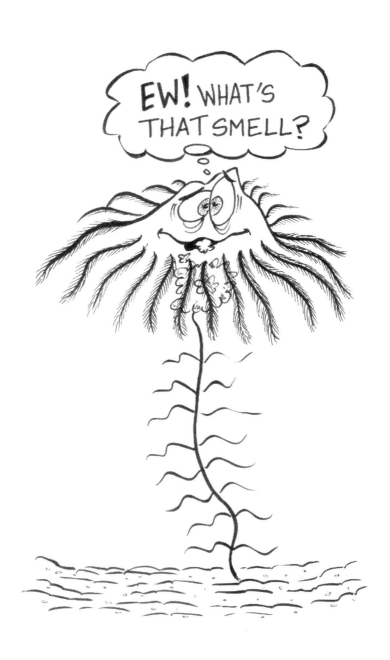

Fart Breathers

ONE ANIMAL FARTS into its own mouth.

A crinoid, also called the Sea Lily, is a sea animal that looks a bit like a plant. Its bottom has grips which hold it onto rocks, which is probably why it doesn't have room for a bum.

The Sea Lily's intestine is U-shaped, and its mouth and its anus are right beside each other on its face.

And, yes, they do fart. Right in their own faces.

Beetle Love Farts

WHEN A GIRL Southern Pine Beetle is looking for love, she farts, and the boy beetles come running.

A female holds gas in her bum which contains a pheromone: that's a chemical whose smell attracts the opposite sex. When she finds a comfortable pine tree to land on, she farts it out, and the nearest males buzz on over.

In fact, her farts can get a big party started. The pheromone, called frontalin, actually attracts both male and female beetles, with a message that means, "Come over to my tree, and let's hang out and eat bark together."

Southern Pine Beetle dinner parties must be a real gas.

Maggot Fart Medicine

MAGGOT FARTS MIGHT be as good as antibiotics.

Researchers in Singapore have discovered that maggot flatulence kills the bacteria which can infect open wounds.

That means, next time you get a cut, forget plasters or antiseptic cream. Just spray on some maggot farts!

Cockroach Farts

IS THERE ANYTHING more disgusting than cockroach farts?

How about *studying* cockroach farts? There have been not just one, but many scientific experiments involving cockroach flatulence.

In 1991, scientists at Michigan State University in the USA studied the effects of different foods on cockroach emissions. The discovered that cockroaches fart more when they eat dry dog food than when they eat corn on the cob. Now you know!

In 1994, Dutch scientists compared roach, beetle, insect, and spider farts, and made the astounding discovery that cockroaches fart less than termites. They were estimating how much methane in the atmosphere is created by various bugs. The answer: quite a lot!

But they didn't answer the most obvious question: which bug farts are the funniest?

SECTION FIVE

FARTS IN THE NEWS

Fart Wars

IN 1994 SWEDEN and Russia nearly went to war over fish farts.

Swedish defence forces picked up underwater clicking noises in Stockholm Harbour which sounded like Russian submarine signals. The Swedish Navy went on high alert, while their Prime Minister sent an urgent, angry message to the Russian President. Yet there was no submarine to be found.

It turned out the little clicking noises were herring farts (see the page about "Fish Fart Language").

Sweden did not declare war against the farting fish.

Fart Contests

IN MOST CONTESTS, the participants who stink usually lose. But not in these:

The First Annual San Francisco Farting Contest took place in 1989. It was apparently also the last. The champion farter won US$500.

The Mamelodi Fart Competition took place in a South African shopping mall on 7 May 2016. Contestants were given boiled eggs and castor oil to help them along.

Instead of a judge, a "farting technician" judged the entries by their sounds. According to the organizer, the purpose of the competition was to encourage young people to break the drug habit by breaking wind instead.

Next: an official Olympic event?

Emergency Farts

IN 2015, SHEEP farts forced an aeroplane to make an emergency landing.

A Singapore Airlines cargo plane flying from Australia to Malaysia was halfway through the flight when the smoke alarms went off. After making an emergency landing on the Indonesian island of Bali, they discovered the "smoke" was actually accumulated farts from the two thousand sheep on board.

Farts on Fire

ON 15 APRIL 2016, a Japanese hospital patient set herself on fire with a fart.

Surgeons at Tokyo Medical University Hospital were operating on the woman with a laser scalpel. In the middle of surgery she farted, which the laser accidentally ignited. The resulting burst of flame burnt the patient's lower body and set the operating room curtains on fire.

Hopefully, beans were removed from the hospital food menu after that.

Illegal Cow Farts

IT IS AGAINST the law for cows to fart in California.

In September 2016 the US State of California passed a law to fight global warming by reducing the amount of methane emitted by farm animals. Under this law, cow farts and poop must be, um, *wiped* out.

Perhaps they should copy what dairy farmers in Argentina are doing: strap on special cow backpacks which collect their animals' farts into bags. At the end of each day, the collected methane is used as biofuel.

Or, since cows fart from front and back (see "Cows Fart at Both Ends"), maybe put a giant plug in one end, to reduce methane emissions by half.

Farts on Trial

IS THE RIGHT to fart protected by law? It depends who does the smelling.

IN 2012 A New Jersey man pointed a gun at his neighbour for farting outside his apartment. The man with the gun was arrested. The right to fart wins over the right to bear arms.

IN 2014 THE Case Pork Roll company, also in New Jersey, fired a man for stinking up the office with his "extreme gas and uncontrollable diarrhoea." His wife sued the company for discrimination against farters. The judge dismissed the case. One can only imagine how the evidence was presented.

A FLORIDA WOMAN was arrested in December of 2015 for assaulting her husband because he farted too much.

At first she kicked him out of bed for stinking up the room. When he returned and continued to cut the cheese, she kicked and punched him so violently that the police showed up and arrested her.

Let's hope her cellmate is on a bean-free diet.

IN OCTOBER 2016, a man in northeast England went on trial for farting in a boy's face. The man was charged with having "wilfully ill-treated the child, namely by breaking wind in his face, in a manner likely to cause him unnecessary suffering or injury to health."

The trial continues, preferably with good ventilation.

Fart Protest

MOST POLITICIANS SPEAK hot air out their mouths. But in the USA some use the other end.

The world's largest "Fart-In" took place at the 2016 Democratic Party national convention in Philadelphia, where Hillary Clinton received the party's nomination for President.

Supporters of the losing candidate, Bernie Sanders, gathered together to eat baked beans before the convention opened, intending to stink up the place in protest. Some "Fart-In" supporters gave out toilet paper, "just in case."

Nobody knows how many people actually voted with their rumps, but organizers claim the protest was "well delivered."

Fart Forecast

THE GASSIEST-EVER WEATHER forecast was broadcast on 4 March 2017, in Jackson, Mississippi, USA.

A boy ran onto the set of the TV weather report and farted right at the weather man. The flustered weather man stood aside while the kid reported on live television:

"There are farts everywhere, and toots."

It was probably the first time in history that a weather forecast was totally accurate.

See the video: youtu.be/myjN5Rb_n94?t=18s

World Record Fart

MANY ONLINE SOURCES claim that Bernard Clemmens of London holds the official Guinness World Record for the longest fart. He supposedly sustained a single fart for 2 minutes and 42 seconds without a break.

Sadly, this is not true. The Guinness World Record office replied to our enquiry: there is no world record category for farting. That really stinks, doesn't it?

The closest we found in the Guinness Book of Records are:

- **The most whoopee cushions sat on in one minute** is 84 and was achieved by Radzi Chinyanganya, in Salford, England, on 10 September 2015.
- **The largest pot of baked beans** contained 5600 litres (1479 gallons), and was achieved by Davcev Stojan in Sarcievo Village, Macedonia, on 7 August 2012.
- **The most baked beans eaten in three minutes** is 166 and was achieved by David Houchin, in Wooton, England, on 23 January 2016. No mention is made of what sounds or smells came out afterward.

FARTS IN HISTORY

Oldest Fart Joke

THE WORLD'S OLDEST joke ever recorded was a fart joke.

It was discovered on tablets written in the ancient land of Sumeria in 1900 BC (almost 4000 years ago), and went like this:

"Something which has never occurred since time immemorial; a young woman did not fart in her husband's lap."

Ancient Greek Farts

BE SMART, DON'T fart.

Pythagoras, the ancient Greek mathematician who invented the Pythagorean Theorem, also created the Pythagorean Maxim. He forbade his followers from eating beans, because when they broke wind, he claimed they were farting out their souls.

Four hundred years later people were still laughing about this. The Roman historian Cicero reported:

"The Pythagoreans prohibited consumption of beans, because that food causes a great flatulence which is contrary to the tranquility of a mind seeking the truth."

Fart Like an Egyptian

ONE ANCIENT EGYPTIAN pharaoh was overthrown because of a fart.

In 570 BC, Pharaoh Apries discovered that one of his generals, Amasis, was planning a revolt. The Pharaoh sent an ambassador to threaten the rebel general. When the ambassador arrived, Amasis lifted his leg and farted at the ambassador, telling him, "Take that back to your master."

No one knows whether the ambassador went back and farted in the Pharaoh's face or just told him about it. Either way, Pharaoh Apries was so angry that he cut off the ambassador's nose and ears.

It turned out that the ambassador was popular among Egyptian citizens. They were so upset at how Pharaoh Apries had treated him, that they decided to support the revolt. Soon after, Amasis took over as the new Pharaoh.

Moral of the story: The fart is mightier than the sword.

Roman Fart Riot

THE DEADLIEST FART in history happened in Jerusalem around the year 50 AD.

A huge crowd had gathered in Jerusalem's main temple to celebrate the Jewish Passover feast, while Roman soldiers stood guard. One soldier bent over, bared his bum at the celebrants, and let out a big, noisy fart. Or, as the ancient historian Josephus wrote:

"He turned his breech to the Jews and spoke such words as you might expect from such a posture."

The people were so enraged, they began hurling stones at the soldiers. The Roman Governor sent in more troops and weapons to put down the riot.

Everyone panicked and tried to escape, but the crowd was so big and the exits so few that they trampled all over each other. In the end, over ten thousand people were crushed to death.

All because of a single fart.

CREPITVS

JVPITER

MARS

God of Farts

THE IDEA OF a God of Farts began as a prank. Medieval Christian writers wanted to make fun of Roman worship of pagan gods. Thus they invented an ancient Roman God of Farts, who they named Crepitus Ventris.

Crepitus ventris literally means 'intestinal noise' in Latin. It was obviously a joke.

Nevertheless, later historians and writers believed it. The Roman god Crepitus Ventris is mentioned by a British historian who lived around the same time as Shakespeare. Later, several famous French authors, including Baudelaire, Voltaire, and the novelist Gustav Flaubert, also referred to Crepitus Ventris in their writing.

Holy Crepitus!

Fart Worship

ONE ANCIENT RELIGION really did believe in the holy power of farts.

Manichaeism believed that "farts release divine light from the body." In other words, farting is kind of like prayer, but from the other end.

Manichaeism started around 1800 years ago in the Middle East and spread all the way across Europe and Asia.

No wonder it was so popular: it must have been a laugh riot sitting in church.

FARTS AROUND THE WORLD

Japanese Fart Art

THE JAPANESE PUT the *art* in *fart*.

An 800-year-old scroll painting called "The King of Farts" tells a story in pictures–like a graphic novel–about a man named Fukutomi-no-Oribe, who performs fart dances for the rich and famous. His neighbour Toda tries to copy the master flatulator, but instead instead poops in his trousers. The bad guy loses!

Another old painting is called *He-Gassen*, meaning "Fart Wars". The 33-feet (10 metre) long painting features 18 colourful scenes of people battling by shooting farts at each other.

One of the most popular performers in 18th century Tokyo was a man called Kirifuri-hanasaki-otoko, which means "the mist-descending flower-blossom man". His show consisted of gulping in air and releasing it out the other end in musical "flatulent arias".

Japan's love of artful farts has never gone away. A Japanese TV advert, showing a boy farting in the bath, won an international advertising award. Watch it here:

www.youtube.com/watch?v=LN20e0g8Juk

Chinese Fart Doctors

IN CHINA, YOU can get a job as a professional fart smeller!

These fart doctors analyse your health by sniffing your rectal gas. If your farts are extremely stinky, it indicates an infection in your bowels. A fishy or meaty smelling bum blast could signal bleeding or tumours. And garlic or onion tinted squealer is a warning of inflammation in your intestines. Sweet, bitter, or savoury anal aromas have other diagnoses.

Not just anyone can apply for this pungent position. You'll need to pass nose tests, and go through a rigorous course in smell recognition before you receive your licence as a Professional Gas Smeller (that's the actual term for it). If you pass the test, you can earn up to US$50,000 (£40,000) a year.

First thing you must learn is the Chinese word for fart: 屁, which is pronounced *pì* or *pee*. It's made up of two parts: 尸, which is meant to be a person squatting, and 比, which represents the sound *pee*. So, someone squatting while letting out a high-pitched sound below. Makes sense!

Fart Criminals in Malawi

BREAKING WIND IS breaking the law in the African country of Malawi.

The 2011 Malawian Air Fouling Legislation states: "Any person who vitiates the atmosphere in any place so as to make it noxious to the public, to the health of persons in general dwelling or carrying on business in the neighbourhood, or passing along a public way, shall be guilty of a misdemeanour."

Does this really mean farting is illegal, both indoors and outdoors? The country's Minister of Justice, a Yale Law School graduate, confirmed that it's true. He advised people who don't want a criminal record: "Just go to the toilet when you feel like farting."

The next question is, how will the police train their sniffer dogs?

Toot Hello in the Amazon

IMAGINE LIVING IN a place where farting is the most polite thing you can do.

The Yanomami tribe, who inhabit rain forests in Brazil and Venezuela, fart at each other when they want to say hello.

We'd like to know how they answer the phone.

German Fart Music

GERMANY, THE LAND of Beethoven, is famous for another kind of music.

In many restaurants, if you order a plate of bread and cheese, the waiter might ask, "With or without music?"

He isn't talking about oompah brass bands. He's asking whether you want onions with it. The music comes later...out your bottom end.

Next on the menu you might find Orchestra Soup. This is another name for onion soup, which describes its additional entertainment benefits.

Finally, a popular dish in the Frankfurt area is called Hand Cheese with Music. This is a soft, smelly cheese, with chopped onions sprinkled on top. Fittingly, it is often eaten with pumpernickel bread (see the page about pumpernickel in the Farty Foods section).

No wonder Germany produced so many of the world's greatest musicians.

Fartland's Got Talent

THE 2016 WINNER of *Finland's Got Talent* was Antton Puonti, who was declared the most talented person in Finland for singing popular songs by making fart noises with his mouth.

Fly the Farty Skies

PEOPLE FART MORE while flying. The reduced air pressure in aeroplane cabins makes gases expand. That includes the gas in your intestines. Your farts can increase in volume by thirty percent!

Farting is safest if you're flying in economy class. The fabric seat covers absorb up to half of a fart's smell. First class leather seats don't offer this advantage.

So, should you just hold it in?

Doctors warn that holding back farts while flying can cause indigestion and heartburn. And of course it's hard to concentrate on that movie, book, or game.

Anyway, most people aboard aren't holding it in. By the time you've crossed the country, you've breathed in about 200 farts.

So feel free to let 'em rip...unless you're the pilot.

A European study warned that if the pilot lets loose a stinker within the cramped, air-tight cockpit, the "co-pilot may be affected by its odour, which reduces safety onboard the flight."

So now you know: that turbulence you feel might be coming from *inside* the plane!

Zero-G Gastronauts

ASTRONAUTS FART MORE in space.

That's because in zero gravity, the air in their stomachs can't rise and come out as burps. The burp gas mixes with fart gas in their stomachs, and the digestive muscles push it all out the back end.

Which brings up the obvious question on the next page.

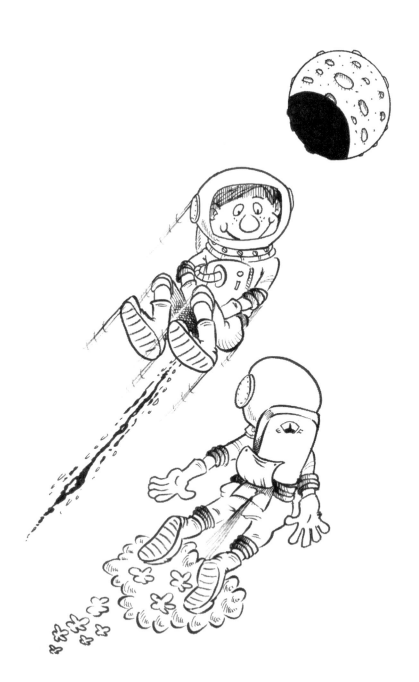

Fart Rockets

DO FARTS ACT like natural rocket engines in space? The universe needs to know!

When asked whether space explorers actually tried blasting themselves through the air by farting, astronaut Chris Hadfield replied:

"We all tried it. Not the right type of propulsive nozzle."

The fact is, farts do have some propulsive force. In zero gravity and the vacuum of space, you could theoretically fart yourself all the way to the Moon...in 300,000 years.

But don't despair! Urinating creates a stronger force than farting (yes, people have actually studied this). Thus, you can travel to the Moon 500 times faster by peeing instead.

116

Space Fart Pollution

NASA SCIENTISTS WORRY that farts in space are truly silent-but-deadly.

Besides stinking up spaceships, the methane and hydrogen in astronaut bum gas can actually be a fire hazard.

In 1969 researchers at the University of California studied how to reduce astronaut farts. They put together two groups of people. One group was fed a diet similar to the menu on the Gemini space missions, and the other was given bland Earth meals. Then they tested their burps and farts.

Not surprisingly, bland food produced less gas.

The study also looked at "psychic and somatic conditions that affect the gut."

Meaning: nervous farts.

In other words, anything that might stress out astronauts—like, say, running into a Death Star, or aliens popping out of their chests—will cause them to fart more.

First Fart on the Moon

ASTRONAUTS FIRST TOUCHED down on the lunar surface in July 1969. But the first confirmed fart on the Moon didn't happen until April 1972.

Apollo 16 astronaut John Young not only farted up a storm while on the Moon, he told the whole universe about it. During a conversation with NASA Mission Control, broadcast live all around the world, Young announced:

"I have the farts again. I got 'em again, Charlie."

FART THESAURUS

Other Words for Fart

Crepitus
Flatulate
Flatulence

Flatus
Gas
Intestinal gas

6.8 on the rectum scale
Air bagel
Air biscuit
Airbrush the boxers
Air tulip
Anal acoustics
Anal 'ahem'
Anal audio
Anal exhale
Anal salute
Anal volcano
Anus applause
Answering the call of
  the wild burrito
Arse acoustics
Arse biscuit
Arse flapper
Back blast
Back draft

Back door breeze
Back door sneeze
Back-end blowout
Backfire
Bake an air biscuit
Baking brownies
Bark
Barking spider
Barn burner
Bean blower
Beef
Beefer
Beep your horn
Belch from behind
Belching clown
Benchwarmer
Better open a window
Blast
Blast the chair

Blat
Blow ass
Blow mud
Blow the big brown horn
Blue dart
Blurp
Blurt
Bomber
Boom-boom
Booty bomb
Booty cough
Bottom blast
Bottom burp
Booty belch
Bowel howl
Break the sound barrier
Break wind
Breath of fresh air
Breezer
Brown cloud
Brown dart
Brown haze
Brown horn brass band
Brown thunder
Bubbler
Bull snort
Bum bazooka
Bum bleat
Bum bongos
Bum burp

Bum cheek screech
Bum dumpling
Bum percussion
Bum sneeze
Bum trauma
Bum trumpet
Bum tuba
Bum yodelling
Bumsen burner
Bun shaker
Bung blast
Burning rubber
Burner
Burp out the wrong end
Buster
Buttock bassoon
Chair air
Cheek flapper
Cheek squeak
Cheeser
Cheesin'
Colon bowlin'
Colonic Calliope
Crack a rat
Crack concert
Crack one off
Crack splitters
Crap call
Crop dusting
Crowd killer

Cut a stinker
Cut one
Cut the cheese
Death breath
Death breeze
Deflating
Doing the one cheek
  sneak
Doing the two cheek
  sneak
Drifter
Drop a bomb
Droppin' stink bombs
Duck call
Eggy
Emptying the tank
Exhume the dinner
  corpse
Exploding bottom
Exterminator
Faecal fume
False pooper
Fanny beep
Fanny frog
Fire a Stink torpedo
Fire in the hole
Firing the retro rocket
Fizzler
Flame thrower
Flamer

Flapper
Flipper
Float an air biscuit
Floater
Floof
Fluffer
Fluffy
Fogger
Fog horn
Fog slicer
Fowl howl
Fragrant foof
Free jacuzzi
Freep
Free speech
Frump
Fumigating
Funky roller
Gas attack
Gas blaster
Gas master
Gasser
Ghost turd
Gluteal maximus gas a
  mess
Gluteal tuba
Gorp
Great brown cloud
Grundle rumble
Grunt

Gurgler
Heinie hiccup
Heinous Anus
Hisser
Hole flapper
Honk
Honker
Horton hears a poo
Hot wind
Hottie
Human hydrogen bomb
Humorrhoids
Ignition
Insane in the methane
Inverted burp
Jet power
Jet propulsion
Jockey burner
Just calling your name
Just keeping warm
Kaboomer
Killing the canary
Lay an egg
Lean mean bean
  machine
Let each bean be heard
Let one fly
Let one go
Let one rip
Let the beans out

Lethal cloud
Let Polly out of jail
Make a stink
Mating call
Methane bomb
Methane dart
Methane mating call
Methane pain
Mexican (food) jet
  propulsion
Moon gas
Mouse on a motorcycle
Mud duck
Nasty cough
Nose death
Odour bubble
Odourama
One-cheek sneak
One-gun salute
One-man band
One-man brass band
One-man salute
Orchestra practice
O-ring oboe
Painting the lift
Paint peeler
Paint stainer
Panty burp
Parp
Parper

Party in your pants
Pass gas
Pass wind
Peter
Pewie
Pip
Playing the tuba
Playing the trouser tuba
Poof
Poof-poof
Poop gas
Poop gopher
Poot
Pootsa
Pop
Pop a fluffy
Pop tart
Power puff
Puffer
Puff the Magic Dragon
Putt-putt
Quack
Quaker
Raspberry
Rattler
Rebuilding the ozone
  layer
Rectal honk
Rectal shout
Rectal tremor

Rectal turbulence
Release a squeaker
Release the hounds
Rip one
Ripped the cheese
Ripper
Ripple
Roar from the rear
Roast the jockeys
Room clearer
Rump ripper
Rump roar
Saluting my shorts
Scud missile
Shoot the cannon
Silent and scentless
Silent and violent
Silent but deadly
Silly cyanide
Singe the chair
Singe the pants
Skunk bait
Slider
Sphincter siren
Sphincter song
Sphincter whistle
Spit a brick
Spitter
Split the seam
Squeaker

Squeak one out
Squidgy
Stale wind
Steam-press your pants
Steamer
Step on a duck
Step on a frog
Stink bomb
Stink burger
Stink it up
Stinker
Stinky
Strangling the stank
  monkey
Stress release
Tail wind
Taint tickle
Testing in the Levi
  wind tunnel
The toothless one speaks
Thunder down under
Thurp
Toilet tune

Toot
Toot your own horn
Tootsie
Trouser cough
Trouser trumpet
Trump
Trunk bunk
Turd tremors
Turtle burp
Tushy tickler
Uncorked one
Uncorking
Under burp
Under thunder
Venting
Vent one
Wallop
Wallpaper peeler
Whiff
Whiffer
Whoopee
Whopper
Zinger

References

Faster than a Flying Fart
www.sciencealert.com/watch-could-you-outrun-a-fart

Gas Warfare
www.craveonline.com/mandatory/1056166-12-very-interesting-facts-about-farts

Fart Breath
scicurious.scientopia.org/2013/05/17/friday-weird-science-whats-your-farting-frequency

Fartometer
www.researchgate.net/publication/225437406_The_quantity_of_colonic_flatus_excreted_by_the_normal_individual

Fart Medicine
www.exeter.ac.uk/news/research/title_393168_en.html

www.theglobeandmail.com/life/health-and-fitness/health/how-a-fart-pill-could-potentially-do-wonders-for-human-health/article33923080

Fart Psychology
www.tandfonline.com/doi/full/10.3402/mehd.v27.30971

Blowiest Beans
www.webmd.com/digestive-disorders/news/20111123/all-beans-arent-the-same-in-gassy-side-effects#1

about.spud.com/blog-gassiest-bean

Fartiest Foods
www.active.com/articles/dietdetective-com-food-and-gas

www.verywell.com/most-gassy-foods-1944687

Stink Sandwich
wikipedia.org/wiki/Pumpernickel

Boy vs Girl Farts
www.realclearscience.com/blog/2014/10/6_facts_you_need_to_know_about_farts.html

Dreamy Farts
www.snorenation.com/stop-farting-in-sleep

Underwater Farts
www.prodiversstkitts.com/pages/divewithus/faq.html

Fart-Free Animals
www.popsci.com/environment/article/2009-05/it-true-birds-cant-fart

Farting Ninja Elephants
www.youtube.com/watch?v=18ilAoVaJFk

Snake Farts
www.livescience.com/43938-coral-snakes-colors-bites-farts-facts.html

Fish Fart Language
news.nationalgeographic.com/news/2003/11/1110_031110_herringfarts.html

Fart Breathers
wikipedia.org/wiki/Crinoid

Beetle Love Farts
www.treesearch.fs.fed.us/pubs/download/39020.pdf

Maggot Fart Medicine
www.iol.co.za/lifestyle/health/maggot-farts-to-the-rescue-486957

www.ncbi.nlm.nih.gov/pmc/articles/PMC3044109

Cockroach Farts
aem.asm.org/content/57/9/2628.short

www.pnas.org/content/91/12/5441.full.pdf

Fart Wars
modernnotion.com/that-time-sweden-and-russia-almost-went-to-war-over-fish-farts-herring-farting

Fart Contests
www.schoolofabsurdity.com/farting-contest

www.sowetanlive.co.za/news/2016/04/22/farters-to-compete-in-mamelodi-contest

www.timeslive.co.za/lifestyle/2016/05/09/WATCH-Farting-to-help-kick-the-drug-habit

Emergency Farts
avherald.com/h?article=48e6ef9c

Farts on Fire
www.asahi.com/ajw/articles/AJ201610300030.html

Illegal Cow Farts
nypost.com/2016/09/21/it-will-soon-be-illegal-for-cows-to-fart-in-california

www.good.is/articles/backpack-collects-cow-farts

Farts on Trial
www.newser.com/story/149006/cops-guy-threatened-gassy-neighbor-with-gun.html

lawnewz.com/crazy/someone-tried-to-sue-company-after-allegedly-firing-worker-for-farting

www.nydailynews.com/news/national/florida-woman-assaults-husband-farting-bed-article-1.2474111

www.thesun.co.uk/news/2013106/roofer-goes-on-trial-accused-of-wilfully-mistreating-a-child-under-sixteen-by-deliberately-farting-in-his-face

Fart Protest
www.usnews.com/news/articles/2016-07-27/anti-clinton-fart-in-makes-stink-at-dnc-gates

Fart Like an Egyptian
www.reshafim.org.il/ad/egypt/herodotus/apries.htm

Roman Fart Riot
modernnotion.com/the-roman-fart-that-sparked-a-deadly-riot

God of Farts
en.wikipedia.org/wiki/Crepitus_(mythology)

Japanese Fart Art
www.atlasobscura.com/articles/the-true-story-of-roland-the-farter-and-how-the-internet-killed-professional-flatulence

en.wikipedia.org/wiki/He-gassen

Chinese Fart Doctors
gizmodo.com/5966617/job-opportunity-how-about-an-exciting-career-as-a-professional-fart-smeller

Fart Criminals in Malawi
en.wikipedia.org/wiki/2011_Malawian_Air_Fouling_Legislation

www.dailymail.co.uk/news/article-1351174/African-country-set-make-breaking-wind-crime.html

www.youtube.com/watch?v=FiBDUa-lFpM

Fartland's Got Talent
www.youtube.com/watch?v=HA_rxemmR48

Fly the Farty Skies
consumerist.com/2013/02/15/yes-theres-a-study-about-passing-gas-on-planes-let-it-rip-unless-youre-the-pilot/

Fart Rockets
www.news.com.au/technology/science/retired-astronaut-answers-amazing-questions-about-space/story-fnjwlcze-1226776314758

www.youtube.com/watch?v=iaN0xg2VQSo

Space Fart Pollution
www.ncbi.nlm.nih.gov/pubmed/12197533

First Fart on the Moon
io9.gizmodo.com/5907904/the-time-an-apollo-16-astronaut-swore-about-farting-on-the-moon

Thesaurus

www.flatulencesolutions.com/fart-euphemisms/

www.huffingtonpost.com/ben-applebaum/different-words-for-fart_b_3498191.html

*Even girls are allowed!

Who writes this stuff?

M.D. WHALEN (writer)

He was always the kid who sat in the back of the class scribbling stories and cartoons. Later he sat in front of the class scribbling stories, when he should have been teaching! Now he writes full time in the back of his house, and has published many books under other names. He also enjoys cycling, world travel, and making rude noises in different languages.

DES CAMPBELL (artist)

Brought up on British comics—Beano, Whizzer & Chips and such—Des has always drawn daft cartoons. He tries to be sophisticated and cultured, but it's all big noses, wonky teeth and funny feet... that's also how his characters look!

Be a smarter farter with more Farty Facts!

Plants fart. Kids go to prison for farting. Moth farts can kill, but kangaroo farts might save the planet. The most famous farters in history. Pump up your Fart IQ, impress your friends and teachers with this gas-powered second volume of funny and Farty Facts.

Know the facts?
Now read the stories!

Can Willy and Peter defeat the evil clowns and save all humanity from ex-*stink*-tion with Weapons of Mass Flatulation?

Willy and Peter blast their way into space. But do they have enough gas in their guts to repel an invasion of farting aliens from Uranus?

Printed in Great Britain
by Amazon